CHINESE MYTHOLOGY

Mazu
Goddess of the Sea

BY SUE GAGLIARDI

CONTENT CONSULTANT
GANG LIU, PhD
ASSOCIATE TEACHING PROFESSOR
CARNEGIE MELLON UNIVERSITY

Kids Core
An Imprint of Abdo Publishing
abdobooks.com

abdobooks.com

Published by Abdo Publishing, a division of ABDO, PO Box 398166, Minneapolis, Minnesota 55439. Copyright © 2023 by Abdo Consulting Group, Inc. International copyrights reserved in all countries. No part of this book may be reproduced in any form without written permission from the publisher. Kids Core™ is a trademark and logo of Abdo Publishing.

Printed in the United States of America, North Mankato, Minnesota.
102022
012023

Cover Photo: Mark Brandon/Shutterstock Images
Interior Photos: iStockphoto, 4–5, 28 (bottom); Shutterstock Images, 7, 16, 28 (top); Mr. and Mrs. Dissevelt-van Vloten/ Rijksmuseum, 8; Keren Su/China Span/Alamy, 10, 20–21, 26; Wang Dongming/China News Service/Getty Images, 12–13, 29 (top); Universal Education/Universal Images Group/Getty Images, 14; Red Line Editorial, 15; Ivan/Moment Open/Getty Images, 18; Cavan Images/Getty Images, 22, 29 (bottom); Taiwan Formosa/Alamy, 25

Editor: Ann Schwab
Series Designer: Ryan Gale

Library of Congress Control Number: 2022940787

Publisher's Cataloging-in-Publication Data

Names: Gagliardi, Sue, author.
Title: Mazu: Goddess of the Sea / by Sue Gagliardi
Description: Minneapolis, Minnesota: Abdo Publishing, 2023 | Series: Chinese Mythology | Includes online resources and index.
Identifiers: ISBN 9781532199967 (lib. bdg.) | ISBN 9781098275167 (ebook)
Subjects: LCSH: Deities--Juvenile literature. | Gods, Chinese--Juvenile literature. | Mythology, Chinese--Juvenile literature.
Classification: DDC 299.51--dc23

CONTENTS

While Lin Mo began life as a human, she later became Mazu, the goddess of the sea.

CHAPTER 1

Goddess of the Sea

Long ago, a young girl named Lin Mo lived in ancient China. Lin Mo had a special gift. She could see the future in her dreams. Sometimes Lin Mo went into **trances**. Her dreams and trances revealed dangers at sea.

One story about Lin Mo tells how she fell into a trance. She had a vision of her father and four brothers at sea. They were swept off their boat during a fierce storm.

Lin Mo used her powers to rescue them. She took a spirit form and went to the sea. She pulled her father and three of her brothers to safety. But just as she reached for her fourth brother, her mother touched her. Suddenly, Lin Mo woke from her trance. At that moment, she lost her grip on her brother. He fell into the sea and drowned.

Lin Mo was known to have special powers. As Mazu, she is worshipped by many people.

Mazu protects travelers from storms at sea.

Lin Mo was very sad. She climbed to the top of a mountain. As she looked down at the sea, she was **transformed** into a beam of light. As her light touched the clouds, a rainbow formed. From that day on, Lin Mo started to become famous. Over time, her legend grew and she became Mazu, the goddess of the sea.

A Goddess for the People

Even after she became a goddess, Mazu stayed on Earth to help people. She protects humans and brings them knowledge. Fishers and travelers look to her for protection at sea.

Chinese Mythology

In ancient China, people told **myths** to explain
their world. Many Chinese myths feature gods
and goddesses. Some stories tell how gods
help farmers grow crops. Other stories tell

how the world was created and why the stars stay in the sky. Many Chinese myths tell of gods who control the weather. These gods protect people from floods and storms. Some myths explain how writing was invented. Many stories feature dragons and other mythological creatures. These myths were passed down from generation to generation. Some stories told of the sea goddess, Mazu.

Explore Online

Visit the website below. Does it give any new information about mythology that wasn't in Chapter One?

Mythology

abdocorelibrary.com/mazu

Thousands of people attend a festival held each year celebrating Mazu's birthday. The event features many dancers and musicians.

CHAPTER 2

The Story of Mazu

Mazu was a human before she became a goddess. She was called Lin Mo when she was a human girl. When Lin Mo was born, she never cried. As she grew older, she never spoke. People called her Mo Niang, which means "Silent Girl."

In one version of her story, Lin Mo was born
to a poor fishing family. Her mother's name was
Wang. Her father was Lin Yuan. Lin Mo was the
youngest child and the only girl in the family.
She had four older brothers. It is said that Lin
Mo lived on Meizhou Island during the 900s CE.
This island is located close to the southeast
coast of China.

Mazu's Home

According to the myths, Lin Mo was born as a human child in 960 CE on Meizhou Island in China.

Guanyin is a goddess connected to Mazu. Guanyin is honored as a goddess of compassion, mercy, and kindness.

Lin Mo was very kind and compassionate. She was always willing to help people. She knew about weather and the stars. Lin Mo used her knowledge to predict storms. She knew about medicine and was a healer in her town.

Goddesses of Kindness

Mazu is known for her kindness. Other Chinese goddesses are also known for being friendly, generous, and considerate of others. Mazu has a special connection with Guanyin, the goddess of compassion. Guanyin is believed to have helped Lin Mo's mother give birth.

Mazu is popular in China as well as in other nearby countries, such as Malaysia and Vietnam.

After Lin Mo died, stories about her became popular. She became famous. Over time, she became known as Mazu or Matsu, goddess of the sea. The name Mazu means "mother" and "ancestor." Many people still look to Mazu for her kindness and protection.

Mazu and the Dragon

Some myths about Mazu feature a dragon. Stories say that a dragon rose from the sea. The dragon gave Lin Mo a bronze coin. The coin is what gave Lin Mo her mysterious powers. This is how she gained the power to heal people. The coin also allowed her to predict the weather. Lin Mo had the power to calm storms. She warned fishers of storms at sea.

Further Evidence

Look at the website below. Does it give any new evidence to support Chapter Two?

Mazu

abdocorelibrary.com/mazu

Mazu is usually shown wearing sparkling jewelry.

Mazu in Art and Culture

In art, Mazu is often shown wearing a bright robe. Her robes are full of shiny jewels. The jewels help fishers and sailors see her from a distance when they are at sea.

A giant statue of Mazu overlooks China's southern coast, offering protection to fishers and sea travelers.

Some artwork shows Mazu holding a tablet. The tablet is a symbol of her knowledge. Mazu also wears a headdress. This headdress shows that she is a goddess. Artists paint pictures and carve statues to honor Mazu. Statues of Mazu watch over seafarers along China's coast.

Mazu's Temples

People build **temples** to honor Mazu. More than 4,000 temples devoted to Mazu exist around the world, including in the United States. People pray for her protection when they travel by sea. In the past, many families made long sea journeys when they moved to another country. After they arrived safely, they often built a temple to Mazu. The main Mazu temple is on Meizhou Island. More than 160 million people around the world honor Mazu.

Safety at Sea

Fishing is an important part of Chinese culture. Fish symbolize good luck and wealth. Some myths explain how gods taught people to fish. Fishers and sailors feel Mazu's protection. Some stories say she has appeared on a chariot of clouds to rescue people stranded at sea. Other myths say Mazu can push huge waves aside so ships can pass safely.

Goddess of the Sea Festivals

Many people take part in festivals to honor Mazu. The festivals feature a religious ceremony and procession. People celebrate Mazu through music, dancing, and puppetry. Opera singers honor Mazu with their voices.

Many people wear costumes when they take part in
the festivals that honor Mazu.

Mazu is a **deity**. People pray to Mazu for peace, protection, and good luck. In some Chinese traditions, fishers and farmers carry lanterns as they walk and pray for peace. They believe that Mazu protects them from the dangers of nature. She is honored as a symbol of mercy and love.

PRIMARY SOURCE

Zhang Zhijun is a Chinese politician. He spoke at a ceremony honoring Mazu. He explained how honoring Mazu brings people together.

> We share the same language and the same beliefs. We are a family on the same boat for the same voyage.

Source: Zhuan Ti. "Mutual Respect in Worship of Mazu." *China Daily*, 16 June 2014, chinadaily.com.cn. Accessed 24 Mar. 2022.

Point of View

What is the author's point of view on this topic? What is your point of view? Write a paragraph about how they are similar or different.

LEGENDARY FACTS

As goddess of the sea, Mazu protects fishers and travelers at sea.

There are thousands of temples honoring Mazu around the world.

Mazu is honored at festivals. People worship Mazu and pray for her protection.

Statues of Mazu watch over seafarers along the coast of China.

Glossary

culture
the way of life of a group of people, including their traditions, beliefs, and art

deity
a god or a goddess

myths
traditional stories or legends that explain the history or cultural beliefs of a group of people

procession
a group of individuals moving along in an orderly way, often done during a ceremony

temple
a building that people use for religious worship

trance
a dreamlike state

transformed
changed in shape or appearance

Online Resources

To learn more about Mazu and Chinese mythology, visit our free resource websites below.

Visit **abdocorelibrary.com** or scan this QR code for free Common Core resources for teachers and students, including vetted activities, multimedia, and booklinks, for deeper subject comprehension.

Visit **abdobooklinks.com** or scan this QR code for free additional online weblinks for further learning. These links are routinely monitored and updated to provide the most current information available.

Learn More

Bell, Samantha S. *Dragons of Chinese Mythology.* Abdo, 2023.

Fu, Shelley. *Chinese Myths and Legends: The Monkey King and Other Adventures.* Tuttle, 2018.

Index

About the Author

Sue Gagliardi writes fiction, nonfiction, and poetry for children. She enjoys exploring myths of cultures from around the world. She lives in Pennsylvania with her husband and son.